Sugar Gliders

Julie Murray

Abdo
NOCTURNAL ANIMALS
Kids

abdopublishing.com

Published by Abdo Kids, a division of ABDO, PO Box 398166, Minneapolis, Minnesota 55439.
Copyright © 2018 by Abdo Consulting Group, Inc. International copyrights reserved in all countries.
No part of this book may be reproduced in any form without written permission from the publisher.

Printed in the United States of America, North Mankato, Minnesota.

102017

012018

 THIS BOOK CONTAINS
RECYCLED MATERIALS

Photo Credits: Alamy, iStock, Science Source, Shutterstock

Production Contributors: Teddy Borth, Jennie Forsberg, Grace Hansen

Design Contributors: Christina Doffing, Candice Keimig, Dorothy Toth

Publisher's Cataloging-in-Publication Data

Names: Murray, Julie, author.

Title: Sugar gliders / by Julie Murray.

Description: Minneapolis, Minnesota : Abdo Kids, 2018. | Series: Nocturnal animals |
         Includes glossary, index and online resource (page 24).

Identifiers: LCCN 2017908182 | ISBN 9781532104077 (lib.bdg.) | ISBN 9781532105197 (ebook) |
         ISBN 9781532105753 (Read-to-me ebook)

Subjects: LCSH: Sugar gliders--Juvenile literature. | Nocturnal animals--Juvenile literature. |
         Marsupials--Health--Juvenile literature.

Classification: DDC 599.2--dc23

LC record available at https://lccn.loc.gov/2017908182

Table of Contents

Sugar Gliders

Sugar gliders live mainly in Australia.

Australia

5

They have soft **fur**. Most are gray. Their bellies are cream.

They have black stripes.

They are small. They only weigh five ounces (142 g)!

They have big eyes. They can see well in the dark.

They have nests in trees. They sleep during the day. They look for food at night.

They glide from tree to tree.

Their skin acts like a kite!

They have long tails. The tail steers them in the air.

They like to eat sweet foods.
They eat tree sap. They also
eat **nectar**.

Features of Sugar Gliders

large eyes

long tail

sharp claws

stripe down back

Glossary

fur
the short, fine, soft hair of some animals.

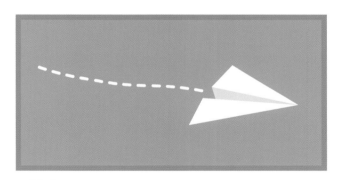

glide
an unpowered, smooth flight.

nectar
the sweet liquid a plant makes.

Index

Abdo Kids
ONLINE
FREE! ONLINE MULTIMEDIA RESOURCES

Visit **abdokids.com** and use this code to access crafts, games, videos, and more!

Abdo Kids Code:
NSK4077